Personal Action Guide

Success from the Inside Out

Insights, Tools and Resources from Steven Rowell,
The IDEA Doctor®

Table of Contents

10 Steps to a Strong Personal Foundation

1. **Honor your boundaries.**
   Boundaries protect you from people your spirit cannot easily afford.

2. **Raise your standards.**
   The higher your standards, the fewer problems you will experience in life.

3. **Clarify your requirements.**
   All those in your life deserve to know what you expect or require of them.

4. **Finish your unfinished business.**
   The fewer unresolved items in your life, the more confident you will feel.

5. **Get your personal needs met.**
   Until your personal needs are met, it's difficult to live powerfully and sustainably.

6. **Orient around your values.**
   When you orient your life and your goals around your values, fulfillment naturally occurs.

7. **Build reserves in all areas.**
   Having more than enough calms the mind and affords more experimentation in life.

8. **Identify and reduce tolerations.**
   What you put up with drains your energy and slows your development.

9. **Handle the money, completely.**
   Until your money is handled, you are not at choice in life.

10. **Define success for yourself.**
    When you define success for yourself, life becomes very, very simple.

Things to Consider in Addressing Each Area

1. **Honor your boundaries.**

Boundaries protect you from people your spirit cannot easily afford.

Boundaries keep us healthy—emotionally, spiritually, behaviorally, physically, and mentally. This is true at work and in our personal lives.

Some workplace examples of boundaries for Leaders to keep in check:

✓ You are the boss, not the employees' buddies—no matter how hard this may be for you to maintain. If you are a manager and you attend an after-hours function with your own employees, you are instantly putting yourself at risk of blurring the boundaries of boss-employee relationships. Your presence alone can send a signal to some employees that the event is "company sponsored." Be very careful. If you must attend an after-hours function, especially when alcohol is being served, simply refuse any alcoholic beverages and depart the function as early as is appropriate for your level of leadership in the organization. If you believe you "must" consume an alcoholic beverage, consume ONLY one, period. Unfortunately you must exhibit the same self-control when it comes to dancing. Only dance one or two dances, and never do so with an alcoholic beverage in your hand.

✓ **Never** initiate an after-hours function by yourself for your peer managers AND subordinates to attend together.

✓ If you are leading the coordination of an after-hours function, make sure it is only a company-sponsored event and that this fact is crystal clear to everyone.

✓ **Never** fraternize or date one of your subordinates, period. If you find yourself "absolutely convinced" this person is the soul mate with whom you are going to spend the rest of your life, then change the working relationship between the two of you FIRST, even before the first date or "friend's lunch." This can be extremely difficult, but, yes, one of you must change jobs if your work relationship is manager-subordinate. Dating peers is as much a problem in my book as well.

✓ Be extremely wary of ever giving or loaning money to your employees. No matter how "inspired" or "called" to give the money you may believe you are, you cannot cross this boundary. As soon as you loan or gift money to a single subordinate, you may be perceived as "showing favoritism" by other subordinates. You will lose this battle in the tabloids, the gossip mill, and your own hallways, EVERY TIME. **Instead of** gifting or loaning money to your staff, connect your team member with organizations or other people who can provide solutions, including money, services, or products. Borrowing from an age-old parable, I paraphrase, "Teaching your staff how to fish is far better for everyone than just handing a fish to your staff members." Your role as Leader is to support, but it is more important to teach and develop the thinking of your staff. This professional development is the leadership gift that will stay with your staff for a lifetime.

✓ Consistently strive to keep your personal values in check with your organization's values and expectations. It's only true Leaders who refuse to do something asked of them by their employer if the employer's request is significantly contrary to the Leaders' personal value system. This single issue has been known to keep people up for hours and days at a time, struggling with: What is the right thing to do? Compromising your personal values at work "just to keep your job" is one of the most painful, potentially damaging, if not destructive, situations Leaders deal with at work. The price is heavy; the results take time to measure. And the inner conflict of the unresolved issue can stick with you forever.

✓ Failing to significantly, consistently lead the forward progress of your department, program, or service week to week, while continuing to cash your paycheck, is a violation of the ethical commitment Leaders make to their employer. Either own your limitations and begin to lead your program, or own your situation and resign. I have personal effectiveness coaching clients who have struggled with this scenario in their own minds for years. This unresolved internal conflict can become a gigantic energy drain, to the point of causing serious personal issues. Honor your boundaries as a Leader, an employee, a peer, and as a subordinate within your own organization.

2. Raise your standards.

The higher your standards, the fewer problems you will experience in life.

Setting your standards high AND then living, performing, or executing at this level minimizes the problems you will experience in life with others simply because you will be operating at a higher level of performance altogether. You will still have problems though. They will be more complex or sophisticated problems, but indeed, there will be fewer of them. It is simply a natural law of our lives that the greater success one achieves, the greater the problems one faces. On the morning Donald Trump walked in the rain alone at 3:00 a.m. to negotiate bankruptcy settlement with an international banker, he passed a homeless person on the street. Being $1 billion in debt and facing bankruptcy, Trump realized the homeless person was $1 Billion richer than he was. This was a turning point in his realization of the magnitude of his current situation.

When you set higher standards for yourself, you operate at a much higher level. Think about the common experience of the busy manager who finally decides to fix, once and for all, his own obesity problem.

Making the choice to change eating habits, sleep habits, and exercise habits collectively serves the person to begin living at a much healthier level. This new level of health increases his energy, focus, endurance, and longevity, while helping him manage stress and lower the risk for heart disease and other chronic illnesses. He will experience fewer health problems, but new problems will surface, such as balancing workout time with work and family time.

3. Clarify your requirements.

All those in your life deserve to know what you expect or require of them.

If you watch any episode of the new television shows *Super Nanny* or *Nanny 911*, you will witness, time and again, that children want and need to know what is expected of them by their parents, and want and need to be held accountable when they fail to meet these expectations. It's so true. As a new father, I am learning these life lessons on a daily basis. Similar to setting and honoring healthy boundaries, people must own what they truly need and then clearly express this to the people in their lives.

When it comes to expectations and requirements, adults are nothing but babies with big bodies. They want the same clarity in expectations and requirements, especially from their bosses at work.

✓ You will struggle to effectively clarify your requirements personally and professionally until you have clarified your own values and defined purpose for your life and for your work. A few great resources for this personal work include *The Purpose Driven Life* by Rick Warren; *Seven Habits of Highly Effective People* and *The 8th Habit,* both by Stephen Covey; *Self Matters* by Dr. Phil McGraw.

✓ You must be clear about your beliefs, attitudes, and biases as well. Knowing what you believe is the first step. Searching for understanding of why you believe what you believe in beliefs, attitudes, and biases is the personal journey that many of us will struggle with the rest of our lives. To assist you with this, I offer you the following list of areas to consider as you "get real" about your beliefs.

1. Define your beliefs of what it means to be a great Leader in your current work situation—as specifically as possible.
2. What are your beliefs about your own industry, your own department, your employer, your organization, your customers, your employees?
3. What do you think about young people, older people, those who are physically challenged, mentally challenged, emotionally disturbed, psychologically disturbed, wealthy, poor, educated, undereducated, Southerners, Northerners, union workers, non-union workers, clinical care givers, nurses, non-clinical department employees, senior executives, middle managers, and front-line workers?
4. What are your hot buttons in dealing with: customers, clients, employees, patients, family members, bosses, peers?
5. What gives you the greatest joy in your work?
6. What gives you the greatest angst, stress, and lack of joy in your work?
7. How did you end up in this current job? What beliefs are guiding you to respond this way to the previous question?
8. What is your legacy? Why are you here? Why are you working here? Why are you doing what you are doing?

✓ After you are clear about your values, attitudes, and beliefs, what are your personal and professional requirements at work?

- ✓ What do you need from yourself to succeed at work? From your staff? From your managers?

- ✓ How and when are you going to communicate these expectations and requirements? And with whom are you sharing these?

- ✓ Here are some examples of clarifying your requirements at work as a Leader:

    1. How you want to receive feedback and/or coaching.
    2. Your definition of personal accountability.
    3. What are the rules of the game as they apply to decision making, performance, team play, autonomy, roles, and discipline?
    4. List your behavioral standards for each role or your department.
    5. Your definition of what it means for your staff to be Leaders at work while honoring the importance of being team players and getting along well with everyone on the team.
    6. Your definition of an effective start of a shift, end of a shift, passing on of information between shifts, and ways to clean/stage equipment at the end of each shift.

To assist you, you will want to capture your thoughts and responses in each of the following areas to clarify your requirements.

- ✓ My Values

- ✓ My Purpose in Life

- ✓ My Purpose in Work

- ✓ My Beliefs at Work

- ✓ My Hot Buttons

- ✓ My Greatest Joy

- ✓ My Greatest Stress or Frustrations

- ✓ My Legacy at Work

- ✓ What I need from Others at Work
- ✓ My Requirements for My Work Team

An example of a Leader's responses to this "Clarifying Your Requirements" section follows:

A. My Values (I honor the following)

Honesty	Integrity	Hard Work	Competence	Compassion
Urgency	Service	Attitude	Courage	Accountability
Dignity	Faith	Love	Community	Growth
Discipline	Learning	Generosity	Passion	Fun

B. My Purpose in Life

My gifts of compassion, generosity, belief in the potential of others, passion for learning, storytelling, coaching, facilitation, and training culminate in the purpose of leading others to discover their own truth while achieving their greatest personal and professional potential.

C. My Purpose in Work

My "purpose gifts" enable me to support, coach, mentor, inspire, and train managers to consider and take action toward the goal of becoming the most effective leaders and members of community possible.

D. My Beliefs at Work

Today's young people (under 25) have less commitment to paying dues and working hard than previous generations. Unions are outdated, ineffective as currently practiced, entities that need to be abolished completely. This will only be possible with more effective management and leadership in place consistently throughout the country.

All people are capable of being racist, sexist, prejudiced, discriminatory, biased, and hateful toward other groups of people perceived as different from them. Most people lack or at least fail to exhibit the courage and maturity required to say what they truly think or feel to their boss or co-workers. A vast majority of service workers such as housekeepers and laundry workers believe they tend to not be respected by almost all people working in the other departments of an organization.

Leadership is the art and craft of creating a safe enough environment where employees believe in the trust of their fellow co-workers and bosses, which in turn allows employees to achieve greater productivity, business outcomes, and service results for the benefit of the organization.

E. My Hot Buttons

People who lie and cheat; people who don't carry their own workload; gossips, instigators, or negaholics. Immaturity and selfishness.

F. My Greatest Joy

My greatest joy at work is when people professionally and personally grow because of the work we have shared together, and they appreciate my coaching, mentoring, or support in their own journey. The greatest moment is realizing when people begin to believe more in themselves than even I had believed in them and then watching them achieve truly incredible things in their lives because of their own strong self-belief.

G. My Greatest Stress or Frustrations

Balancing financial and people decisions simultaneously. Dealing with conflict and facing people in order to resolve conflict.

H. My Legacy at Work

I built a team of people who operate a department as well (if not better) in my absence than in my presence. Mine became the department with the highest employee satisfaction and lowest turnover rates consistently for more than three years in a row.

I. What I need from Others at Work

I need people to bring the same level of focus, maturity, professionalism, and passion for excellence to their work as I do.

J. My Requirements for My Work Team

My team will "own" the start and end of their shifts by providing proper pass-on log information, setting up equipment for the incoming shift, and managing their own schedule changes. My team members will achieve a level of professionalism so they can interact with our key users themselves without leaning on their supervisors or managers to conduct a meaningful, results-oriented conversation with consistent follow through.

4. Finish your unfinished business.

The fewer unresolved items in your life, the more confident you will feel.

Carrying unfinished business is a major energy drain for most people. The solution to this issue at work is to resolve conflicts, disagreements, misunderstandings, or unfinished situations as quickly and completely as possible. Some examples to use at the beginning of your work day or work week are:

✓ Ask yourself and make as complete a list as possible of the following:

- What are you mad, glad, or sad about at work or with someone or some situation?
- What are you going to stop, start, or continue doing in order to "finish your business" rather than leaving it unfinished?
- What are all the benefits to you and to others around you when you address the situation, concern, person, or conflict that is unresolved?

✓ Own your life and do only those things that keep you on track to finish your unfinished business:

- If possible, commit to never leave work on your "Friday" with unresolved issues or situations.
- Or commit to having any unfinished business resolved within x number of days, so you can move on, hopefully, in a healthy way.
- Acknowledge when you need help and ask for it.

Examples of issues or situations to consider worth "finishing" are:

- Forgiving someone.
- Resolving hurt feelings from a previous experience or conversation.
- Admitting your mistakes to make room for the relationship to improve.
- Letting go in a healthy way.
- Writing a letter to someone who has passed.
- Apologizing even when you don't know if it will make a difference.
- Listening to someone else's perspective without interruption, after having argued vehemently about this issue previously.

- Committing to live in the now, letting go of the past, and not focusing too much on the future—live in the now.
- Resolving arguments or hurt feelings with parents, children, family members, bosses, peers, or subordinates.

5. **Get your personal needs met.**

Until your personal needs are met, it's difficult to live powerfully and sustainably.

Stop denying yourself what you need to achieve a healthy, stable, powerful life. First, you must identify what your personal needs are.

You must be sure to fulfill all of your personal safety needs first before taking on the burden, challenge, or joy of other aspects of life if you are to achieve your full, true potential.

Be selfish in a healthy way! Doing things for yourself is actually a healthy practice as long as it is not overdone. Frankly, some of the healthiest, most balanced Leaders I have ever met speak about this level of selfishness as being one of the top three critical skills for their success, specifically in the area of balancing work with private and family time.

6. **Orient around your values.**

When you orient your life and your goals around your values, fulfillment naturally occurs.

What matters most to you? What are you willing to defend? Iraqi citizens recently were willing to risk death from flying bullets or explosives in order to practice their new right to vote, yet we struggle to get Americans to vote every year—even in presidential elections.

Both your personal power (self-confidence) and your courage are based largely upon your values. Therefore, clarity in identifying these values keeps them far closer to the forefront of your thinking and your daily experience in a constructive way.

Build reserves in all areas. Having more than enough calms the mind and affords more experimentation in life.

This is so true. Think about how you feel when you have plenty of sleep or how you feel when you know you have money in savings, even if it's only $500. Make a list of areas in which you need to build reserves.

For example:

- Savings account
- Available credit on one credit card for emergencies
- Space in the garage that is free of clutter
- Stored food for when supplies run low
- Batteries and flashlights for emergencies at home
- An old-fashioned telephone that is powered by the phone line, in case your power goes out and all your "modern" telephones don't work
- Daily exercise for extra strength and increased energy
- "Emotional deposits" in the "banks" of your friends, co-workers, team members, children, spouse, or partner so that you have something to withdraw on those days when you need their support or help (best to make these deposits before taking withdrawals)

7. Identify and reduce tolerations.

What you put up with drains your energy and slows your development.

Handle the money, completely. Until your money is handled, you are not at choice in life.

If you truly want to change your life for good as it relates to the way you see money and handle money, then I URGE you to read the following two books:

Rich Dad, Poor Dad by Robert Kiyosaki

Secrets of the Millionaire Mind by T. Harv Eker

Forget about wanting to be a millionaire or billionaire for now. Just read these two books if you want to gain real power over how you see money, how you think about it, and how you spend or save it.

8. Define success for yourself.
When you define success for yourself, life becomes very, very simple.

Of all of the personal coaching I have done over the years, this is the single most important thing people must do in order to take action and begin building the life they truly want.

Until you define success for yourself, you are at the whim of everyone else—your boss, friends, spouse, children, co-workers, and others.

Here are some powerful questions to answer that will help you get to your own definition of success:

- ✓ Where do you see yourself one year from today? (Be as specific as possible.)
- ✓ What gives you your greatest joy at work or in your personal life?
- ✓ Where do you see yourself five years from today? (Be as specific as possible.)
- ✓ In the past 30 days, what specifically have you done to achieve anything related to any of these previous three questions?
- ✓ Over the next 30 days, what specifically do you have to do to begin achieving your definition of success?
- ✓ And the big question: What are all the outcomes and/or benefits to you when you achieve this definition of success? (If this list doesn't excite you, then you may need to look at your definition again.)
- ✓ What is your legacy? How do you want to be remembered?

Quality of Life 100

Instructions:

1. Check the box if the statement is consistently true for you.
2. If the statement doesn't apply to you, please change the language so that it does, or replace it with a different statement that fits within the category. Then evaluate the new statement as in step 1.
3. Add up your section scores and your total score.
4. Check back every 30 or 90 days and you will likely see progress, even if you aren't focusing directly on this program.
5. Work with a coach to help you get through the challenging times.

1. Family & Relationships

- ☐ I am both pleased and content with my spouse/partner, or happy being single.
- ☐ I am close to my parents, alive or not. There is nothing in the way or between us.
- ☐ I have a circle of friends I truly enjoy, without any effort.
- ☐ I have a best friend and treat him/her extremely well.
- ☐ I am very close to my children. There is nothing in the way.
- ☐ I enjoy my family/extended family; we have worked through any dysfunction and past problems.
- ☐ I am part of a professional network that stimulates me intellectually and emotionally.
- ☐ I get along well with my neighbors.
- ☐ I have at least 20 friends and colleagues who live outside of my country of residence.
- ☐ I am loved by the people who mean the most to me.

____ Section Score (Number of checked boxes)

2. Career & Business

- ☐ My work/career is both fulfilling and nourishing to me; I am not drained.
- ☐ I am highly regarded for my expertise by my manager, clients, and colleagues.
- ☐ I am on a positive career path that leads to increased opportunities and raises.
- ☐ I work in the right industry or field; it has a bright future.

- ☐ I usually look forward to going to work every day.
- ☐ My work is not my life, but it is a rich part of my life.
- ☐ I work with the right people.
- ☐ My work environment brings out the very best of me because it is wonderfully stimulating and/or very supportive.
- ☐ At the end of the day, I have as much energy as I did when I started the day. I am not drained.
- ☐ The work I do helps to meet my intellectual, social, and/or emotional needs.

____ Section Score (Number of checked boxes)

3. Money & Finances

- ☐ I have enough money in the bank or a money market fund to at least cover a year's living expenses.
- ☐ I am on a financial independence track or am already there.
- ☐ I don't have to work at financial success; money seems to find me with very little effort or pushing.
- ☐ I have no financial stress of any kind in my life.
- ☐ I invest at least 10% of my income/earnings in my ability to increase/expand that income.
- ☐ I do not carry credit card debt; I do not overspend.
- ☐ When I buy something, I buy the best possible quality.
- ☐ I don't lose sleep over my investments.
- ☐ I am financially knowledgeable in that I know how money is made and lost.
- ☐ I make money because I provide more than enough value to the people/customers who need what I have.

____ Section Score (Number of checked boxes)

4. Joy & Delight

- ☐ I spend my leisure time totally enjoying my interests; I am never bored.
- ☐ Weekends (or other days off) are a joy for me.
- ☐ I have designed the perfect way to spend the last hour of my day.
- ☐ I usually look forward to getting up every morning.

- ☐ I am very, very happy.
- ☐ I have designed—and am living—the perfect lifestyle for me right now.
- ☐ I have at least an hour a day that is exclusively for me; I spend it in a chosen way.
- ☐ I am able to stay present during the day; I don't lose myself to stress or adrenaline.
- ☐ I easily take delight in the smallest things.
- ☐ My home brings me joy every time I walk inside.

____ Section Score (Number of checked boxes)

5. Effectiveness & Efficiency

- ☐ I don't spend time with anyone who bugs me or who is using me.
- ☐ I have more than enough energy and vitality to get through the day without dragging.
- ☐ I have no problem asking for exactly what I want from anyone.
- ☐ I have all of the right tools, equipment, computers, software, and peripherals that I need to work well.
- ☐ Whatever can be automated is automated.
- ☐ Whatever can be delegated is delegated.
- ☐ I reply to all emails as I read them, and I don't maintain an inventory of unanswered emails.
- ☐ I don't put things off; when it occurs to me, I do it, handle it, or have it done.
- ☐ I know what my goals are, and I am eagerly and effectively realizing them.
- ☐ I don't do errands, except by exception.

____ Section Score (Number of checked boxes)

6. Responsibility & Foundation

- ☐ I love my home (location, style, furnishings, light, and feeling).
- ☐ My boundaries are strong enough that people respect me, my needs, and what I want.
- ☐ I tolerate very, very little; I'm just not willing to.
- ☐ I don't see a cloud on my future's horizon; it looks clear.

- ☐ My wants have been satisfied; there is little I want.
- ☐ My personal needs have been satisfied; I am not driven or motivated by unmet needs.
- ☐ There is nothing I am dreading or avoiding.
- ☐ My personal values are clear; I am oriented around them.
- ☐ I have resolved the stresses and key issues of my upbringing and past events.
- ☐ I don't have a lot of unfinished projects, business or hanging items; I am caught up.

____ Section Score (Number of checked boxes)

7. Personal Development & Evolution

- ☐ I could die this afternoon with no regrets.
- ☐ I am living my life, not the life that someone else designed for me or expected of me.
- ☐ There is nothing that I am not facing head-on; nothing I am putting off dealing with.
- ☐ I attract success; I don't have to strive for it or chase it.
- ☐ I have more than enough natural motivation, inspiration, and synergy in my life. I am not stuck.
- ☐ I am evolving, not just improving, because I continually experiment.
- ☐ I have progressed beyond the notion of beliefs.
- ☐ I am at that place in life where I initiate and cause events, not wait for others to do so.
- ☐ I have learned to take the path of least resistance as I accomplish my goals.
- ☐ I am beyond striving for success; I simply enjoy life and focus on what fulfills me.

____ Section Score (Number of checked boxes)

8. Self-Care & Vitality

- ☐ I take at least 4 vacations per year.
- ☐ Life is easy; I have almost no problems or unresolved matters affecting me.
- ☐ My teeth and gums look great and are in top condition.

- ☐ I have more than enough time during my day.
- ☐ I eat food for sustenance and pleasure, not for emotional comfort.
- ☐ I am not abusing my body with too much alcohol, television, caffeine, or drugs.
- ☐ Whatever health problems I have, I am receiving proper, effective care for them.
- ☐ My body is in great shape.
- ☐ I reduce stress daily by meditating, taking a long bath, exercising, walking, etc.
- ☐ There is nothing I am doing that is messing up my mind or heart.

____ Section Score (Number of checked boxes)

9. Happiness & Contentment

Please write down 10 situations, routines or scenarios that make, or would make, you the happiest and most content.

- ☐ ______________________________
- ☐ ______________________________
- ☐ ______________________________
- ☐ ______________________________
- ☐ ______________________________
- ☐ ______________________________
- ☐ ______________________________
- ☐ ______________________________
- ☐ ______________________________

- ☐ ______________________________

Now re-read the list and check the boxes of those that exist for you now.

____ Section Score (Number of checked boxes)

10. Pleasure & Excitement

Please write down 10 activities that you truly enjoy, whether you currently do these things in your life or not.

- ☐ ______________________________
- ☐ ______________________________
- ☐ ______________________________
- ☐ ______________________________
- ☐ ______________________________
- ☐ ______________________________
- ☐ ______________________________
- ☐ ______________________________
- ☐ ______________________________
- ☐ ______________________________

Now re-read the list and check the boxes of those that exist for you now.

____ Section Score (Number of checked boxes)

____ TOTAL SCORE (Total of all Section Scores—100 is highest possible Total)

Scoring Key:

90-100 Congratulations. Awesome. Incredible.

80-89 Excellent! Your score is very high—this is a tough test.

70-79 Very good. You're definitely on track. Keep going.

60-69 Pretty good, but there is some work to do.

50-59 Average Score. Why not make your quality of life a priority and score 10 more points in the next month?

40-49 You may need to make some important changes.

30-39 Support yourself. You deserve it. Why not make yourself a priority!

00-29 Hello? Anybody home?

Energy Drains

What are you tolerating or putting up with that drains your energy? Make a list of at least 25 things that you are tolerating in your life.

We put up with, accept, take on, and are dragged down by people's behavior, situations, unmet needs, crossed boundaries, incomplete efforts, problems, and even our own behavior (avoidance, silence, compliance). You are putting up with more than you may think, so what are you tolerating in your life right now? Be specific.

1. ______________________________

2. ______________________________

3. ______________________________

4. ______________________________

5. ______________________________

6. ______________________________

7. ______________________________

8. ______________________________

9. ______________________________

10. ______________________________

11. ______________________________

12. ______________________________

13. ______________________________

14. ______________________________

15. ______________________________

16. ______________________________

17. ______________________________

18. ______________________________

19. ______________________________

20. ______________________________

21. ______________________________

22. ______________________________

23. ______________________________

24. ______________________________

25. ______________________________

What are you willing to do to change? What is this costing you right now?

Exercise: Identify the first eight of these tolerations that you will eliminate or at least decrease within the next 30 days.

Energy Drains

What are you tolerating that drains your energy? Make a list of at least 20 things that you are tolerating in your life.

We put up with, accept, take on and are dragged down by people's behavior, situations, unmet needs, crossed boundaries, incomplete efforts, problems, and even our own behavior (avoidance, silence, compliance). You are putting up with more than you may think, so what are you tolerating in your life right now? Be specific.

✓ 1. My living arrangements

✓ 2. Lack of storage space at home

✓ 3. Unorganized/unusable garage at home

✓ 4. My weight

✓ 5. My job not being satisfying, rewarding or challenging anymore

✓ 6. Financial worries

✓ 7. Too much spending on luxury items

✓ 8. Foot pain that I keep avoiding/not dealing with

✓ 9. Self-doubt about my . . .

✓ 10. Procrastinating on completing my taxes

✓ 11. Not cleaning up the backyard storage shed

✓ 12. Not dealing with car repairs

✓ 13. Credit card debt out of control

✓ 14. Arguing with my spouse

- ✓ 15. Worrying about the future rather than focusing on the present
- ✓ 16. Messy office work space
- ✓ 17. Too many emails stored without responding to them
- ✓ 18. Too much unresolved mail at home
- ✓ 19. Dirty laundry in the back bathroom (avoiding)
- ✓ 20. Disappointment about no longer attending church
- ✓ 21. Going out too many evenings each week with friends
- ✓ 22. Not enough sleep
- ✓ 23. Not exercising
- ✓ 24. Unresolved anger with . . .
- ✓ 25. Not dealing directly with . . .

What are you willing to do to change? What is this costing you right now?

Exercise: On the back of this page, identify the first eight of these tolerations that you will eliminate or at least decrease within the next 30 days.

For each item you are eliminating, you need to come up with a list of what you will STOP doing to eliminate this item, and START doing, and CONTINUE doing.

Stop, Start, Continue and Mad, Glad, and Sad

Two of the more powerful and effective tools I share with my clients for them to use in facilitating team meetings and individual meetings as well are, Stop, Start, Continue and Mad, Glad, and Sad.

Some of the most common situations to use these tools in are:

- ✓ Teambuilding with staff or management teams
- ✓ Soliciting feedback from front-line staff
- ✓ Facilitating constructive coaching conversations with an individual
- ✓ Having discussions with almost anyone when your need is to discover the "real issues" of a situation or a relationship

Stop, Start, Continue and Mad, Glad, and Sad can be completed in private by groups of individuals, in dialogue with an individual, or as an interactive team exercise for an entire team simultaneously (using flipcharts for data capture).

A traditional example of using Stop, Start, Continue with a group of employees is to pass one copy of the Stop, Start, Continue form to each participant. Then ask everyone to quietly read through the handout and privately write down their responses to the following questions using the Stop, Start, Continue handout. You could then facilitate a group discussion, asking individual participants to share whatever they are comfortable sharing in discussion with the entire group.

This Stop, Start, Continue form can be used with individuals in private one-on-one conversations as well in an effort to offer a tool to guide your discussion. You could send the form to the person in advance of your meeting as well if this makes your face-to-face time more meaningful and efficient.

Another method of using this Stop, Start, Continue process is to bring a group of 10 to12 employees or managers together. (Traditionally this is not used with managers and staff in the same group—at least in the beginning of your use of this process). Using flipcharts around the room, one labeled STOP, one labeled START, and one labeled CONTINUE, you simply ask everyone to either approach the flipchart pages and write their ideas down under each category, or use Post-it notes first—with one idea written per Post-it, and then ask the participants to place their Post-its on the flipchart pages under each category.

There are advantages and disadvantages to each of these data-collection methods for Stop, Start, Continue (or Mad, Glad, and Sad).

Method One - Ask participants to use markers and write their ideas under each category: STOP, START, CONTINUE.

ADVANTAGES:

- ✓ Participants are able to move around the room at their own will.
- ✓ Participants are able to write down their own thoughts without having to share with the larger group.
- ✓ Data collection tends to be extremely fast due to the fact that people disburse throughout the room—this is especially true for larger groups when you post multiple blank flipchart pages on the walls for each category.
- ✓ Flipchart pages can be easily stored for use later in typing up the data from the meeting

DISADVANTAGES:

- ✓ Participants tend to watch people as they write their comments down on the flipchart pages, which can prove challenging or anxiety provoking for some participants. This contributes to the possibility for group think to occur as well; that is, participants change their responses after seeing what others have begun to write on the various flipcharts. In the extreme, participants become biased by the presence of one or two comments, and they simply follow along with these few statements rather than contribute what they are truly feeling or needing to express.

Method Two - Ask participants to use Post-it Notes, one Post-it per idea, and then have them place each of their Post-it Notes under each category: STOP, START, CONTINUE.

ADVANTAGES:

- ✓ Participants perceive greater privacy, because they fill out each Post-it Note in the room with the group but without letting anyone see what they are writing.

- ✓ Participants get out of their seats to place their Post-it Notes, but again, most cannot see what is written on other people's notes during this process.

- ✓ The use of Post-it Notes allows you or the facilitator to organize the notes quickly under each category in themes, or to consolidate repetitious comments.

- ✓ Repetitious comments can be easily organized by placing Post-it Notes together in a line for each category, which visually shows the frequency of comments for each theme under each category. Some of my clients put the Post-it Notes in columns or rows in order to show the frequencies of each issue, resulting in a bar graph of Post-it Notes or a histogram.

DISADVANTAGES:

- ✓ Once the Post-it Notes are put on the flipchart pages, they are difficult to be read by participants once everyone is seated for discussion. The handwriting tends to be small.

- ✓ After the meeting, the handling of the flipchart pages is a little more tedious because the Post-it Notes can tend to fall off or move as the flipchart pages are folded and used later.

Once your team's data is collected, you can use a variety of methods to have your team prioritize the various themes or ideas under each category: STOP, START and CONTINUE.

A similar process is used to solicit feedback using Mad, Glad, and Sad.

Examples of questions to use in the Stop, Start, Continue exercise are:

- ✓ What could we Stop, Start, or Continue to do together as a department to make this a better place to work?
- ✓ What could I Stop, Start, or Continue to do as your boss to become an even better one?
- ✓ What does each of us need to Stop, Start, or Continue doing in order to become more effective team members?
- ✓ Thinking of the way in which this team communicates on a regular basis, what do we need to Stop, Start or Continue doing?

Examples of questions to use in the Mad, Glad, and Sad exercise are:

- ✓ Thinking of your daily life here at work, what are you Mad about, Glad about, and Sad about?
- ✓ When you think of how our team interacts and supports each other, what are you Mad about, Glad about, and Sad about?
- ✓ When you think of how we treat our customers or patients, what are you Mad about, Glad about, and Sad about?

The only "rules" to use when soliciting feedback from participants using these two tools:

- ✓ If you provide an idea for one category, please offer another idea for the other categories (for example, if you list a Stop, list a Start too; if you list a Mad, list a Glad too).
- ✓ Your contribution must be genuine, constructive, and sensitively worded.

Current Concerns

What am I MAD about?

What am I SAD about?

What am I GLAD about?

What are my priorities to address?

Personal Commitments

What should I STOP doing?

____

____

____

What should I START doing?

____

____

____

What should I CONTINUE doing?

____

____

____

What are the BENFITS to me?

____

____

____

The Group Ladder

Based on Lacoursierre's work in group dynamics as well as the valuable research of many others, the Group Ladder was created to represent the steps or stages that intact work groups experience together.

All groups begin at the first step of Safety. The question group members are asking is "Who am I?" As time goes on, the group will either progress forward and upward in the Group Ladder or become stagnant at a relatively fixed place on the Group Ladder.

In the event of significant change (change of leader, major shift of some sort external to the group or internal to the group) or in the event of significant conflict among the group, the group will revert back to the first step, SAFETY.

How quickly the group returns to its previous position on the ladder depends on the nature of the change or conflict faced by the group, the group's ability to resolve the conflict or manage the change, and the quality of the trust and safety the group had in the first place.

In other words, the amount of safety and trust a group experiences and builds results in the level of strength or stability in the foundation steps of SAFETY and TRUST.

Conflict Resolution Worksheet

The "inability to effectively resolve conflict with another person" is one of the most common topics for which my leadership training participants ask me for help. I have found that the most common reasons for leaders to avoid resolving a conflict are:

- ✓ Perceived lack of skill to resolve the conflict (how to deal with it)
- ✓ Not knowing what to say
- ✓ Fear of losing something, including the relationship
- ✓ Lack of self-confidence to face the struggle
- ✓ Fear of the tension from resolving the conflict
- ✓ Supposed belief that the relationship isn't worth worrying about
- ✓ Lack of time to sit face-to-face with the person to resolve conflict
- ✓ Minimizing the conflict in your head, commonly just an avoidance technique

The first level of conflict resolution is to understand yourself, the other person, and the conflict itself. For example, the first issues to try to be clear about include the following:

- ✓ What is the conflict—its source and its reason for occurring?
- ✓ Why does this conflict matter to you, or how does it currently impact you?
- ✓ What is your behavioral style (such as Platinum Rule styles) and what does that tell you about what you need for this situation to be resolved?
- ✓ Now, answer the previous three questions from the other person's perspective as well.

The next level of conflict resolution is to ask yourself a series of questions which are designed to assist you in gaining greater clarity regarding your conflict with another person. Answer these questions as honestly as you can.

1. What are the possible sources of your conflict?

2. What are all the issues you are trying to resolve?

3. What is keeping you and the other person from being able to resolve the conflict? For you? For the other person?

4. What is the greatest risk you will have to take to face the conflict?

5. How difficult will this risk taking be for you?

6. What are all the benefits that would come from resolving the conflict?

7. Focusing on your internal feelings or physical state, how will you feel after this conflict is resolved?

8. What is the Platinum Rule behavioral style of the other person, and what needs does this person have? (See PlatinumRule.com)

9. What would happen if you did nothing about this situation? Does this result matter to you?

10. How much time per week would you "re-gain" if you were to resolve the conflict once and for all? What negative emotional energy would no longer be used and exhausted when you effectively resolved the situation?

11. Map out (on the back of this page) the various approaches you could take to address the conflict. (Various versions of your first approach; ways to engage the other person; list with as much detail as you wish; what the other person is bound to say or do in the event of a negative reaction; prepare possible responses for each of the possible approaches you may experience.)

The final step is to confront the person with whom you are conflicted or to lead/facilitate the discussion between two people.

What is the Disney Difference?

Leveraging Disney Principles within Your Own Program

Ever since leaving employment with The Walt Disney World Co., I have been asked so many times, "What is the Disney Difference?" or "What makes Disney so successful?" The three areas that people are most intrigued by or interested in are: 1) understanding the secrets to Disney's overall success—organizationally, branding, as an employer; 2) understanding the secrets to Disney leadership principles that make a difference; 3) what it is like to be a "cast member" working for Disney. More recently there has been a fascination with Disney from the health care industry to understand and then leverage Disney principles in an effort to achieve greater patient satisfaction.

Here I will share, for the very first time, an insider's look into the principles that guide Disney's success. I am offering only those practices and principles I believe are relevant for you to consider and reflect upon when you are strategizing your own next steps as a Leader, especially in this industry. I invite you to consider adopting and adapting any of these principles within your own Leadership practice.

Disney's Enduring Principles

1. We Sell Happiness (capture your essence in five words or less).

2. Safety, Courtesy, Show, Efficiency (Four guiding principles. The order does matter; they build upon the previous principle—this is one of the most enduring, unique aspects of Disney because the vision is "complete" encompassing the total process and experience for a cast member and a guest).

3. Walt Disney was a master storyteller. Storytelling is at the core of all Disney does today, whether it's new-hire orientation, training a new hire, welcoming guests to a theme park, guests entering an attraction, or even having dinner at a Disney resort.

4. High-touch refers to building interaction into the guest experience, giving guests the chance to participate, make choices, and interact with the cast. High-show refers to the need to build into the guest experience vivid presentations that are memorable. High-tech refers to the need to build speed, accuracy, and expertise into service delivery, which results in giving your guests the gift of time and cutting-edge products and services. (The creation of FastPass and the ticketing system used at Disney theme parks are examples of high-tech.)

5. Your organization is only as good as your selection process. "Hire for attitude, Train for Skill" is their focus. Quality begins in the recruitment/selection process rather than in the training process. Disney hires people who are already courteous, positive, enthusiastic, and people-oriented rather than waste millions of dollars on teaching people "how to be nice" or "how to smile."

6. In the mid-1990s, Disney redefined career success as laterally transferring and taking on multiple roles over time as more valuable than simply being promoted vertically. This was brilliant for retention, cast-member satisfaction, retaining organizational history by retaining veteran cast members, and minimizing the pressure to grow in terms of attractions and resorts in order to retain "A-talent" cast members.

7. Every guest matters, no matter what.

8. Always, always, always, see the world through the eyes of your guests. Make changes immediately if you discover something wrong.

9. Continually look for barriers to achieving service excellence, identify the barriers, and then eliminate them. Period.

10. Guidelines for guest service include the following: Make eye contact and smile!; greet and welcome each and every guest; seek out guest contact; provide immediate service recovery; display appropriate body language at all times; preserve the "magical" guest experience; and thank each and every guest.

11. "Everything Speaks" means even the smallest details matter. It is in the mastery of the smaller details along with the major details that makes it possible for an organization, a team, or an individual to achieve truly legendary service. Some examples of this include: 1) appropriate, accurate, adequate signage; 2) what does your parking garage look like to your customers?; 3) elevator buttons that are mislabeled and never updated; 4) phone directories that are not kept current; 5) failing to minimize clutter and personal trash within a work area that is visible by guests; 6) employees using language that is most appropriate at all times.

12. "Living our Culture" every day is what makes the place magical. The service we provide within our culture is what is expected by our guests.

13. Disney service is rooted in the magic of show business. Everyone performs a role for the guests. Creating magical memories for guests from the show is each cast member's ultimate responsibility.

14. Language Matters. It is critically important to the culture.

- ✓ Hotels are called Resorts
- ✓ Rides are called Attractions
- ✓ Customers are called Guests
- ✓ Employees are called Cast Members
- ✓ Managers are called Coaches
- ✓ You are either On-stage or Back-stage
- ✓ Buses are Motor Coaches
- ✓ Cast Members are Hosts when speaking with a Guest, e.g., Security Guard is Security Host; Bus Driver is Motor Coach Host; "Ride Operators" are Attractions Hosts
- ✓ No Guests vomit; they have a Protein Spill

Disney Best Practices

- ✓ The Disney Casting Center uses an **eight-minute preview video** with all applicants that helps describe the nature of a day working at Disney. On average, 10-13% of all Job Fair respondents leave the process immediately after the first step of reviewing this video—great best practice to eliminate wrong-fit talent at the beginning of the selection process.

- ✓ New-Hire Orientation, known as **Traditions**, is facilitated by front-line, hourly paid cast members who serve as traditions assistants in a cross-utilization role. They maintain their full-time or part-time positions within the company and serve periodically as traditions assistants.

- ✓ On stage, **trash cans** are positioned no more than 19 paces apart because of the research Disney conducted in the mid-1980s. The company discovered the average guest would drop a piece of trash on the ground after 19 paces if a trash can was not readily available.

- ✓ The **Tele-Cast** is a tri-fold, double-sided, pocket-sized information card that lists all relevant show times, theme park hours, telephone numbers, guest information, and unique information relevant to the current week. It is most useful in assisting cast members who need to answer guests' questions on stage.

- ✓ **Costuming and Disney Look Book** provides grooming guidelines. Additionally, backstage mirrors are in key cast-member locations close to doors leading to on-stage areas. These mirrors are three feet by five feet—large enough to catch your attention as you walk by. This powerfully reinforces how serious the organization is about everyone looking his or her best at all times. Hospitals and hotels have implemented this practice with great success. Examples of Disney grooming standards include the following: men on stage cannot have hair that touches their collar; women must wear only natural tones of eye shadow, no mascara, and earrings smaller than a quarter with no hoop earrings allowed at all; only one ring per hand and no visible tattoos for male or female cast members while they are in costumes on stage.

- ✓ **Telephone scripting** requires a commitment from every cast member to say "Have a Magical Day" to every guest on the telephone just before ending the conversation. It wasn't until three years of consistent success with this property-wide practice that management began to allow evening shift cast members to say "Have a Magical Evening" or "Have a

Magical Night." Consistency in the execution of best practices is at the heart of Disney's magic and success.

✓ **Navigational Directions** are available at every telephone either on stage (such as a front desk of a hotel) or backstage throughout the property—this facilitates the cast members' ability to provide directions to guests or fellow cast members WITHOUT transferring the call or passing on the burden of finding directions to someone else. Again, cast members own the guests' experiences, and they treat fellow cast members as their own guests.

✓ **Magic towel folding** in Disney resort rooms is a surprise that guests find when they return to their rooms after a day at the theme parks. This has become one of the most frequently cited items in guest letters (see the Service Special Report #1 Creative Towel Folding for examples).

Disney Leaders Truly Do It Differently:

- ✓ Disney Leaders actually CAN perform the roles of their subordinates. This comes from Disney's philosophy that its managers are competent in the roles for which they are responsible, as well as Disney's exceptionally high percentage of Leader positions that are filled by internal promotion.

- ✓ Hands-on leadership that includes constant walking around with eyes wide open and seeing from the perspective of the guest is the standard for all Leaders.

- ✓ Even if there is no one present, cast members must never eat, drink, smoke, or chew gum on stage.

- ✓ Cast members must never carry drinks, food, cigarettes, or chewing gum in shirt, jacket, or pants pockets while on stage.

- ✓ Never turn your back to a guest when you are on stage. Disney now embroiders the names of cast members on their lanyards—positioned on the back of the neck—so guests walking up to cast members from behind can call them by name immediately.

- ✓ Never conduct a personal conversation with another cast member on stage whether there are guests within earshot or not.

- ✓ Pick up litter as soon as you see it so that the next guest never sees it. This applies to every cast member from front-line through senior vice presidents and is modeled frequently by all.

- ✓ Personal accountability and the managerial courage required to demonstrate it are honored, expected, trained, modeled, and lived by Leaders (not by all, but by a vast majority).

- ✓ When Disney Leaders leave Disney property for a meal or errands on personal time, they immediately remove their Disney name tags. By contrast, think about how many people eat lunch wearing their name tags at a restaurant near their workplace. Sometimes I have fun with these people by walking up, saying hello, and announcing their names. They can't figure out how I know their names or why they can't seem to remember who I am.

- ✓ As a Leader, you are PART of the show, you are NOT the show.

- ✓ Disney Leaders OWN the experience of their cast members because cast members are the Leader's guests. Every cast member is a potential Disney guest.

- ✓ At company functions, a Disney Leader wearing a Disney name tag will never be seen posing for a photograph with an alcoholic beverage in hand.

- ✓ Disney Leaders own the training of their subordinates. This is not delegated to trainers or others, except in the case of new-hire orientation (known as Traditions) and scheduled management-development programs that are company-wide initiatives.

- ✓ Give your employees the tools they need to deliver exceptional service or perform exceptional work. Simple examples include the following: 1) driving directions to your facility posted at every telephone; 2) pocket guides with all of the most important need-to-know information for employees to share with guests; 3) backstage mirrors mounted on the wall so employees can check themselves one last time before they go on stage.

- ✓ Disney Leaders are only successful when their people are successful. Your role as Leader is to develop your staff while maintaining the show and providing the services required for your guests.

- ✓ Take 5: There is a commitment on the part of managers to "Take 5" minutes with a minimum number of their cast members each day at work. The focus of "Take 5" conversations is to check in with cast members on how things are going and listen for feedback or concerns. This practice directly impacts employees' long-term satisfaction.

Disney's Great Leader Strategies

(Introduced in the 1990s as the Standard for Great Leaders)

1. Design your organizational structure for success—break the mold.
2. Make sure you have the right people in the right jobs.
3. Ensure team members are knowledgeable about their jobs.
4. Make dramatic leaps in quality work and quality service.
5. Implement effective structured processes for getting work done.
6. Explore, probe, and know what is going on in your organization, and act upon the information.
7. Actively observe and react to the performance of your direct reports—take time for recognition, coaching, and counseling.
8. Expand and act upon knowledge and experience of the best service available anywhere.
9. Partner effectively and successfully with staff and other cross-functional partners.
10. Demonstrate a passionate, professional commitment to your job.

The Bottom Line

The culture of the Disney organization is a bundling of Show Business, Everything Speaks, "We Sell Happiness," Guests and Cast Members, "we're only as good as our hiring," Change is Constant, Creating Magical Memories is what it's all about, and Safety, Courtesy, Show and Efficiency lead to Exceeding Guests' Expectations.

The reality is that culture will beat strategy every time when it comes to organizations trying to implement new strategies or techniques mid-stream (any time after the inception of the organization). Therefore, organizations must affect change at the level of culture change rather than simply implementing service excellence strategies or best practices.

In other words, Disney theme parks are so clean and the cast members are so friendly and service oriented because the established, proven, tested culture has expectations.

✓ Before being hired, cast members already demonstrate the "friendly" and "service-oriented" attitude during the interview process.

✓ We are in Show Business, and we all have a role to perform for the sake of our audience of guests.

✓ Each cast member has the opportunity, moment to moment, to either support the Disney culture or to not honor it. Supporting the culture is rewarded, recognized, and expected in hundreds of ways. Cast members bend over and pick up litter as soon as they see it on stage; kneel down on one knee when addressing a child; know that children are never lost, their parents are; take no part in eating, drinking, smoking, or chewing gum on stage.

✓ "We are each a part of the Show" has tremendous power and meaning since it implies a purpose larger than ourselves. Therefore, to be a part of it, no matter how minor the role, is to cherish the awesome responsibility we each have in creating the Magic.

✓ The culture is so strong, so real, so current, and so ever-present that execution and performance are not just expected, it is "our way of life at Disney."

The million dollar challenge is to facilitate culture change and redefine effective leadership within an organization that has failed to achieve Disney's level of quality work and service focus and culture since its inception. This is the critical challenge for any organization: to move from marginal to good, and from good to exceptional.

The Secrets to Effectively Leading Lasting Change in an Organization

--John Kotter, Leading Change

- ✓ Establishing a Sense of Urgency
- ✓ Creating the Guiding Coalition
- ✓ Developing a Vision and Strategy
- ✓ Communicating the Change Vision
- ✓ Empowering Employees for Broad-Based Action
- ✓ Generating Short-Term Wins
- ✓ Consolidating Gains and Producing More Change
- ✓ Anchoring New Approaches in the Culture
- ✓ Errors to Avoid When Leading Change:
- ✓ Allowing Too Much Complacency
- ✓ Failing to Create a Sufficiently Powerful Guiding Coalition
- ✓ Underestimating the Power of Vision
- ✓ Under communicating the Vision by a factor of 10, 100 or 1000
- ✓ Permitting Obstacles to Block the New Vision
- ✓ Failing to Create Short-Term Wins
- ✓ Declaring Victory Too Soon

When Dealing with Me...

1. When dealing with me, you need to honor:

2. When coming to discuss a problem or solution with me, you need to:

3. If you want my support, you need to:

4. Most common ways people can ensure they won't receive this support from me are to:

5. The key to gaining my trust and respect is to:

6. To ensure success in interacting with me, you need to demonstrate:

7. My vision of co-workers effectively interacting with each other includes:

Recommendations for using this tool:

The most powerful way to leverage this tool is to bring your team together and ask each person to complete this handout in private while everyone is gathered together. Once completed, simply begin by asking individuals to share aloud their response to one of the questions (seek responses from as many people as possible for the same question to begin group dialogue). As the facilitator, you will want to begin with the question that you believe will conjure up the greatest conversation relative to the issue(s) you think the team is struggling with presently.

After healthy dialogue and wrapping up your meeting completely, you can ask participants to share the one thing they heard or learned from this discussion that they will take with them and begin to honor or work on immediately.

Additionally, you may choose to ask each participant to turn in their "final" responses one week later with the announcement that you will make copies for everyone of each person's responses. Distribute the team members' responses and then reconvene with a couple of weeks to discuss the results.

The 5 Cs of Trust

The ability to gain and keep trust is a vital factor in influencing others. Research has shown time and again that trust is always a contributing factor in the ability to influence others. When people trust you, trust alone can cause them to accept your message. On the flip side, if they don't trust you, all the evidence, reasoning, facts, or figures in the world won't get them to budge.

Trust can be an ambiguous concept, but certain things are quite clear: You can't get others to trust you unless you trust yourself first. Your message will not be convincing to others unless it's convincing to you. Whenever someone tries to influence us, we ask ourselves, "Can I trust this person? Do I believe him? Are they really concerned about me?" We are less likely to be influenced if we sense the person is driven solely by self-interest.

The Five Cs of Trust

- ✓ Character (Integrity and Honesty)
- ✓ Competence (Knowledge and Ability)
- ✓ Confidence (Conviction and Belief)
- ✓ Credibility (History and Experience)
- ✓ Congruence (Consistency and Harmony)

The Five Cs of Trust listed above will all help you gain the trust you need to have lasting influence. Let me illustrate through a story how these elements work. Imagine you're experiencing extreme tooth pain. You've put off going to the dentist as long as possible, but now nature's telling you your time has run out. You recently relocated, so your previous dentist is 2000 miles away and no longer an option. You ask your new friends and neighbors about their dentists and get the following five responses:

1. My dentist has great **character**. He is one of the most honest people I know. He's not very competent, though. I heard he's famous for sticking the needle completely through your cheek.

   Would you go to this dentist?

2. My dentist is one of the top dentists in the state. He's extremely **competent,** but kind of a crook. He has no character. He's been caught a few times for over billing and also sometimes fills more cavities than you actually have.

   Would you go to this dentist?

3. My dentist doesn't have much **confidence** in his work. One time he said to me, "I've never been very good at reading x-rays. I feel unsure about whether I should give you a root canal or just leave the tooth alone. Look at this x-ray and tell me what you think."

   Would you go to this dentist?

4. I'm not sure my dentist is licensed. I didn't see any degree or diplomas on his wall, and no one seems to know where he went to school. His office doesn't have the latest equipment. He even asked me to pay cash instead of writing a check. He has no **credibility** in my book.

   Would you go to this dentist?

5. My dentist is a nice guy, but he doesn't keep his stories straight. Congruency and **consistency** are not his strong suits. Last year he said I'd probably have to get a root canal on my molar the next time I came in. When I came back, I asked him about the root canal on my molar, and he said, "You don't need a root canal on that tooth. Who told you that?"

Would you go to this dentist?

I'm sure you would spend more time trying to find a dentist who met all five criteria. A deep and lasting sense of trust will not exist without all five characteristics. We know if people are lacking in just one of these areas, it will affect every aspect of their ability to build, gain, and maintain trust.

-Source Unknown

Tips for Designing and Implementing Behavioral Standards

Behavioral Standards are also referred to as Standards of Performance, Performance Standards, or Standards in Practice.

Become crystal clear about what your vision is for implementing these standards, what you are trying to accomplish, and why you are doing it. Seek input from all employees in creating the document. This takes time but is the most valuable aspect of the process for ensuring employee buy-in later, which is priceless.

Align desired behaviors with organizational goals and desired outcomes—make sure the priorities match and ring true.

Review other organizations' Standards of Behavior, and study the successful implementations of others.

Be very specific in your wording. Say exactly what you mean and avoid colloquialisms and jargon. For instance, state, "Make eye contact, smile, and verbally greet all guests who come within five feet of you at any time."

Hold a ceremonial Standards of Behavior "roll out." Have all existing employees sign their commitment to the new Standards.

Hold people accountable when they violate a standard. Model the importance of these standards consistently and endlessly, by senior and middle management.

Create a designated "Standard of the Month." Post and distribute liberally throughout the organization for the first 12 months after initial introduction.
Update the Standards of Behavior over time to keep them current.
Have new applicants sign it right up front. Preview it on your website and job application, review it in the interview process, and then have new hires sign their commitment on their first day of orientation to the company.

Keep your list of Standards to no more than seven with brief, clear descriptions of the behavior expected for each standard.

Sample of Behavioral Standards

Respect
- Patients First is our focus
- Respect and honor our employees and physicians
- Model mutual respect by caregivers and leaders

Privacy and Confidentiality
- Maintain confidentiality of patient information at all times
- Respect the privacy needs of our patients
- Conduct appropriate conversations at all times

Quality
- Provide exceptional clinical care to every patient we serve
- Fully embrace the patient's Right To Know
- Demonstrate commitment to continuous improvement

Professionalism
- Serve as a role model for the company at all times
- Choose your attitude daily, with patients and guests in mind
- Look and act the part of a health care professional always

Safety
- Provide a clean, healthy, and safe environment
- Work smarter, and think safety first

Communication
- Fully explain care procedures to our patients in advance
- Be sensitive to the individual needs of our patients
- Keep patients informed about their care throughout their stay
- Listen to and share information in a timely manner among co-workers

Teamwork
- Provide exceptional responsiveness from our staff
- All share in the commitment to co-workers for effective teamwork
- Support the goals of the organization

Accountability
- Everyone takes pride in the work we do and the services we provide
- Each of us holds ourselves accountable in providing exceptional care to our patients
- Each team member is accountable for his or her own choices

Cultural Sensitivity

- We honor the multicultural diversity of our staff and the community which we serve
- We will speak English in all public areas, especially when interacting with patients, unless our patients or their family members require support in their native language

Service

- Consistently seek out guest and patient contact
- Anticipate the needs of patients and visitors
- Enhance the practice and delivery of every aspect of patient care
- Assist all people with directions and finding a location at any time
- Continually raise the standard of excellence

Red Teams

Red Teams are perfect whenever a group needs objective, critical feedback from internal subject-matter experts in a timely manner in order to refine their final plans.

How it Works:

Any group that has worked to develop new processes, standards, guidelines, methods, strategies, implementation plans, or any other process-oriented content or deliverable can use "Red Teams" as a feedback check-in process prior to the final presentation of their new ideas.

Just prior to the conclusion of a development process, the group will identify a small number of internal (perhaps external too) subject-matter experts who have the ability to hear the group's suggestions and plans and provide meaningful feedback, critiques, or criticism of these plans.

The "Red Team" is invited to sit and listen to the group's presentation. The rules of engagement are for the Red Team to sit quietly during the entire presentation, making no comments and simply taking notes. The only questions that Red Team members can ask at the end of the presentation are clarification questions solely for the purpose of fully understanding the presentation.

After the presentation, the presenting group leaves the room for 30 minutes. The Red Team has 30 minutes to make a list of every conceivable piece of meaningful, constructive, critical feedback with a bias toward identifying the items that were missed by the group or inadequately covered, as well as any other weaknesses or missed opportunities within the presentation content. Additionally, the Red Team is to offer as many varying angles or examples as possible of how this solution will not work with thorough explanation as to why it won't work. The concept here is for the Red Team to "blow as many holes as possible through the existing plan."

At the conclusion of the 30 minutes, the Red Team will identify a representative for their group who will explain the team's list of concerns, suggestions, and criticisms to the group. The group will return to the room to listen to the Red Team's representative explain each of the items. The representative is only to present enough information to make each point clear to the group. There is to be no extended discussion with the representative. After completing the presentation and answering any clarifying questions, the representative simply leaves the group.

At this point, the group determines which of the Red Team's items will be addressed before they make the final presentation of their ideas.

The power of this process is to get critical, thoughtful input in reaction to a group's ideas and solutions with as little defensiveness or debate as possible.

It is critically important that Red Team members who are selected for this process be trustworthy, mature, and responsible and will therefore most likely abide by the rules of engagement. Members of the Red Team are not allowed to discuss the group's ideas or anything about the process with anyone else after the Red Team experience is over.

Recommended Reading List

Truly wealthy people have huge libraries in their homes,
poor people have huge television sets.

- Unknown

Entrepreneurship

✓ *E-Myth Revisited*	Michael Gerber
✓ *Rich Dad Poor Dad*	Robert Kiyosaki
✓ *1000 Things You Never Learned in Business School*	William Yeomans
✓ *What They Don't Teach You at Harvard Business School*	Mark McCormack
✓ *Getting Everything You Can Out of All You've Got*	Jay Abraham
✓ *Guerrilla Marketing*	Jay Conrad Levinson
✓ *Guerrilla Publicity*	Jay Conrad Levinson
✓ *No B.S. Business Success*	Dan Kennedy

Human Resources

✓ *Up is not the Only Way*	Beverly Kaye
✓ *Love 'em or Lose 'em*	Beverly Kaye
✓ *Love it, Don't Leave it*	Beverly Kaye
✓ *Now Discover Your Strengths*	Marcus Buckingham
✓ *The First 90 Days*	Michael Watkins
✓ *The 7 Hidden Reasons Employees Leave*	Leigh Branham
✓ *StrengthsFinder 2.0*	Tom Rath

Leadership

✓ *Creating Magic*	Lee Cockerell
✓ *Ultimate Leadership*	John Maxwell
✓ *21 Irrefutable Laws of Leadership*	John Maxwell
✓ *I Feel Great and You Will Too!*	Pat Croce
✓ *Lead or Get Off the Pot!*	Pat Croce
✓ *Winning*	Jack Welch
✓ *The Leadership Challenge*	Kouzes and Posner
✓ *First Break All the Rules*	Marcus Buckingham
✓ *The Coward's Guide to Conflict*	Tim Ursiny

- ✓ *Execution* Larry Bossidy
- ✓ *Do Right* Lou Holtz
- ✓ *John P. Kotter on What Leaders Really Do* John P. Kotter
- ✓ *The Leader's Voice* Boyd Clarke
- ✓ *Management Mess-Ups* Mark Eppler
- ✓ *Managing Workplace Negativity* Gary S. Topchik.
- ✓ *A Survival Guide for Working with Humans* Gini Graham Scott

Personal Effectiveness

- ✓ *The 4-Hour Workweek* Tim Ferris
- ✓ *The 12 Bad Habits that Hold Good People Back* James Waldroop
- ✓ *Financial Peace* Dave Ramsey
- ✓ *Life Strategies* Phillip C. McGraw, PhD
- ✓ *Self Matters* Phillip C. McGraw, PhD
- ✓ *Family First* Phillip C. McGraw, PhD
- ✓ *Getting the Love You Want* Harville Hendrix, PhD
- ✓ *Body for Life* Bill Phillips
- ✓ *Living a Life That Matters* Harold Kushner
- ✓ *9 Things You Simply Must Do* Henry Cloud
- ✓ *The Purpose Driven Life* Rick Warren
- ✓ *The Seven Habits of Highly Effective People* Stephen Covey
- ✓ *The 8th Habit* Stephen Covey
- ✓ *Prisoners of Our Thoughts* Alex Pattakos
- ✓ *How to Win Friends and Influence People* Dale Carnegie
- ✓ *No B.S. Time Management for Entrepreneurs* Dan Kennedy
- ✓ *The Platinum Rule* Tony Alessandra
- ✓ *Awaken the Giant Within* Tony Robbins
- ✓ *Get the Edge* Tony Robbins
- ✓ *Unleash the Power* Tony Robbins
- ✓ *The Power of Now* Eckhart Tolle
- ✓ *Power of Focus* Mark Victor Hansen
- ✓ *10 Foundations of Motivation* Shawn Doyle
- ✓ *Now Discover Your Strengths* Marcus Buckingham
- ✓ *Getting Things Done!* David Allen
- ✓ *You Can't Shove a Great Life into a Small Dream* Tony Magee
- ✓ *Live What You Love* Bob and Melin Blanchard
- ✓ *I Can Make You Thin* Paul McKenna

Organizational Effectiveness

✓ *Urgency*	John P. Kotter
✓ *The Power of Small*	Linda Thaler
✓ *Built to Last*	Jim Collins
✓ *Good to Great*	Jim Collins
✓ *In Search of Excellence*	Tom Peters
✓ *Passion for Excellence*	Tom Peters
✓ *Thriving on Chaos*	Tom Peters
✓ *Re-imagine!*	Tom Peters
✓ *Change*	John Kotter
✓ *Leading Change*	John Kotter
✓ *Flawless Consulting*	Peter Block
✓ *The Dance of Change*	Peter Senge
✓ *First Break All the Rules*	Marcus Buckingham
✓ *Our Iceberg is Melting*	John Kotter
✓ *Urgency*	John Kotter

Publishing

✓ *Self-Publishing Manual*	Dan Poynter
✓ *From Book to Bestseller*	Penny Sansevieri
✓ *Beyond the Bookstore*	Brian Jud
✓ *Author 101 Series of Books*	Rick Frishman
✓ *Perfect Book Proposal*	Jeff Herman

Sales and Client Relations

✓ *What Your Clients Won't Tell You*	John Gamble
✓ *Why Good Clients Fire Great Companies*	John Gamble
✓ *Spin Selling*	Neil Rackham
✓ *Stop Whining! Start Selling!*	Jeff Blackman
✓ *Winning the Toughest Customer*	Delia Passi
✓ *Wake 'em Up Business Presentations*	Tom Antion
✓ *Buyology*	Martin/Lindstrom

Service

- ✓ *Customer Satisfaction is Worthless, Customer Loyalty is Priceless* — Jeffrey Gitomer
- ✓ *Unleashing Excellence* — Dennis Snow
- ✓ *9 ½ Things You'd Do Differently If Disney Ran Your Hospital* — Fred Lee
- ✓ *Hardwiring Excellence* — Quint Studer
- ✓ *Results that Last* — Quint Studer
- ✓ *Give 'em the Pickle* — Bob Farrell

Success

- ✓ *Dig Your Well Before You're Thirsty* — Harvey Mackay
- ✓ *Think and Grow Rich* — Napoleon Hill
- ✓ *Power Networking* — Marc Kramer
- ✓ *The Tactics of Very Successful People* — B. Eugene Griessman
- ✓ *Secrets of the Millionaire Mind* — T. Harv Eker
- ✓ *Jump Start Your Business Brain* — Doug Hall
- ✓ *The Seven Minute Difference* — Allyson Lewis
- ✓ *The Art of Happiness* — His Holiness Dalai Lama
- ✓ *Winning* — Jack Welch
- ✓ *The Last Lecture* — Randy Pausch
- ✓ *People Are Idiots and I Can Prove It!* — Larry Winget
- ✓ *You're Broke Because You Want to Be!* — Larry Winget
- ✓ *The Answer* — John Assaraf

Marketing

- ✓ Every book (Multiple titles) by — Seth Godin
- ✓ *Irresistible Offer* — Marc Joyner
- ✓ *Selling the Invisible* — Harry Beckwith
- ✓ *The Ultimate Marketing Plan* — Dan Kennedy
- ✓ *No B.S. Direct Marketing* — Dan Kennedy
- ✓ *Ultimate Lead Generation Plan* — Matt Bacak
- ✓ *What's Your Story?* — Matthews and Wacker
- ✓ *The Truth About What Customers Want* — Solomon
- ✓ *The Truth About Creating Brands People Love* — Till/Heckler
- ✓ *Brand Sense* — Martin/Lindstrom
- ✓ *FREE* — Chris Anderson

Favorite Quotes

ACTION

Two little words that can make the difference: START NOW.
(Mary C. Crowley)

It's the action, not the fruit of the action, that's important. You have to do the right thing. It may not be in your power, may not be in your time, that there'll be any fruit. But that doesn't mean you stop doing the right thing. You may never know what results come from your action.
But if you do nothing, the fruit is always nothing.
(Mahatma Gandhi)

To fight fear, act. To increase fear-wait, put off, postpone.
(David J. Schwartz)

Consciousness: That amazing time between naps.
(B. Mellin)

That which is common sense is not always common practice!
(Lou Holtz)

A racehorse has to run; a bird has to fly; an artist has to paint; and a teacher has to teach. There is something in you that you have to do.
(Dr. Phil McGraw)

CHALLENGE

Argue for your limitations, and sure enough, they're yours.
(Richard Bach)

Success is going from failure to failure without loss of enthusiasm.
(Sir Winston Churchill)

Do what you hate every morning before 10:00 a.m.
(Pat Croce)

Do you see problems in every opportunity or opportunity in every problem?
(Dale Carnegie)

Give me a stock clerk with a goal and I'll give you a man who will make history. Give me a man with no goals and I'll give you a stock clerk.
(J.C. Penney)

Obstacles are those frightful things you see when you take your eyes off your goal.
(Hannah More)

Patience and perseverance have a magical effect before which difficulties disappear and obstacles vanish.
(John Quincy Adams)

Write the bad things that are done to you in sand, but write the good things that happen to you on a piece of marble.
(Arabic Proverb)

Always shoot for the stars, if you miss, you're still high in the sky!
(Steven Rowell)

She has spent her life in perpetual motion while standing still.
(Caroline from *A Poor Cousin of the Middle Class*
January 18, 2004 NY Times Magazine
(article about the working poor in America))

The only difference between stumbling blocks and stepping stones is the way in which we use them.
(Unknown)

All organizations are perfectly aligned to get the results they are currently getting.
(Arthur Jones)

CHANGE

If you have the awareness that the whole drama of your life is the result of what you believe and what you believe is not real, then you can begin to change it.
(Don Miguel Ruiz)

Everybody thinks of changing humanity and nobody thinks of changing himself.
(Leo Tolstoy)

People don't argue with their own data.
Making it their own is the art and craft of leadership.
(Steven Rowell)

I skate where the puck is going to be, not where it has been.
(Wayne Gretzky)

If there was one thing you could change immediately, what would it be?
(Steven Rowell)

We must be the change we want to see in the world.
(Mahatma Gandhi)

CHARACTER

The ultimate measure of a man is not where he stands in moments of comfort, but where he stands at times of challenge.
(Martin Luther King, Jr.)

If I take care of my character, my reputation will take care of itself.
(Dwight L. Moody)

In the end, we will remember not the words of our enemies
but the silence of our friends.
(Martin Luther King, Jr.)

You are my friend when you can guard my failure, challenge my thought and celebrate my success.
(Unknown)

If your self-esteem is dependent upon anything external to yourself, you are in big trouble.
(Stephen Covey)

In reading about the lives of great men, I found that the first victory they won was over themselves . . . self-discipline with all of them came first.
(Harry S. Truman)

Life consists in what a person is thinking of all day.
(Ralph Waldo Emerson)

Trust comes not from a particular technique, but from the character of the leader.
(Warren Bennis)

ON BECOMING A LEADER

Two monologues do not make a dialogue.
(Jeff Daly)

Coach in Private. Praise in Public.
(Anonymous)

Is that working for you?
(Dr. Phil McGraw)

The truth will set you free, but first it will piss you off.
(Unknown)

COURAGE

The essence of courage is being willing to feel our heart even in situations that are difficult and painful.
(John Welwood)

What would you attempt to do if you knew you could not fail?
(Dr. Robert Schuller)

DECISION MAKING

The highways of life are full of flat squirrels who couldn't make up their minds.
(Unknown)

If you don't know where you're going, any road will get you there.
(Alice in *Alice in Wonderland*)

I don't care what we CAN'T do, tell me what we can, and how, NOW!
(Walt Disney)

I don't care what your five reasons are that we can't do it or won't do it, I want to know how we CAN do it and the five ways TO DO it!
(Jack Welch)

HAPPINESS

Everyday happiness means getting up in the morning, and you can't wait to finish your breakfast. You can't wait to do your exercises. You can't wait to put on your clothes. You can't wait to get out - and you can't wait to come home, because the soup is hot.
(George Burns)

Only one thing has to change for us to know happiness in our lives: where we focus our attention.
(Greg Anderson)

Life does not have to be perfect to be wonderful.
(Annette Funicello)

Work would be great if it weren't for all the people!
(Anonymous Bumper Sticker)

The more you complain, the longer God makes you live.
(A. Thetus)

Happiness is not having what you want, but wanting what you have.
(Anonymous)

LEADERSHIP

Leadership is like a string. Push it and it goes nowhere.
Pull it and it will follow you everywhere.
(Dwight Eisenhower)

The only test of leadership is that somebody follows.
(Robert Greenleaf)

Seek people who have some balance in their lives, who are fun to hang out with, who like to laugh and who have some non-job priorities which they approach with the same passion that they do their work. Spare me the grim workaholic or the pompous pretentious 'professional';
I'll help them find jobs with my competitor.
(Leadership Secrets of Colin Powell - Principle #11)

Only by realizing that to lead is to serve, can a leader fortify his or her position and bring about a lasting increase in prosperity.
(Robert Greenleaf)

Leadership is the art of getting someone else to do something you want done because he/she wants to do it.
(Dwight Eisenhower)

Outstanding leaders go out of their way to boost the self-esteem of their personnel. If people believe in themselves, it's amazing what they can accomplish.
(Sam Walton)

The ultimate leader is one who is willing to develop people to the point that they eventually surpass him or her in knowledge and ability.
(Fred A. Manske, Jr.)

At work, adults choose to do what they are allowed to do, what they know how to do, what they want to do, or what they are taught to do, but most yearn to be INSPIRED to do! What are you inspiring in the hearts and minds of your people?
(Steven Rowell)

A Fish stinks from the head first.
And my manager doesn't even realize he's the head of the Fish.
(Unknown)

LOVE

Darkness cannot drive out darkness; only light can do that. Hate cannot drive out hate; only love can do that.
(Martin Luther King, Jr.)

We must learn to live together as brothers or perish together as fools.
(Martin Luther King, Jr.)

RECOGNITION

A cow never stops needing to be milked.
(D. Baum)

VISION

What YOU focus upon is what your people will focus upon—Period.
You get what you expect.
(Steven Rowell)

People will support that which they help to create.
(Mary Kay)

Vision is the art of seeing things invisible.
(Jonathan Swift)

The future belongs to those who believe in the beauty of their dreams.
(Eleanor Roosevelt)

People only see what they are prepared to see.
(Ralph Waldo Emerson)

We do not see things as they are. We see them as we are.
(Talmudic Teaching)

How do we intend to win in this business?
(Jack Welch)

Someone's sitting in the shade today because someone
planted a tree a long time ago.
(Warren Buffett)

MISCELLANEOUS

Fortune Magazine May 2003

How's customer service doing? Jeff Bezos of Amazon.com isn't interested in a qualitative answer. He wants to know average customer contacts per order, average time per contact, the breakdown of e-mail vs. telephone contacts, and the total cost to the company of each.

"With most decisions, you can do the research, collect the data and do the math to figure out the right answer. Math-based decisions always trump opinion and judgment," Bezos says. "The trouble with most corporations is that they make judgment-based decisions when data-based decisions could be made. It is very common for debates at Amazon to end with let's go get the data."

Built To Last by Jim Collins and Jerry Porras

Built To Last is a book about the most successful and admired companies of the 20th Century.

The critical question asked by a Built to Last company is not "How well are we doing?" but rather "How can we do better tomorrow than we did today?" They institutionalize this question as a way of life – a habit of mind and action.

There is no ultimate finish line for a Built to Last company. There is no "having made it." There is no point at which they feel they can coast the rest of the way, living off the fruits of their labor. In short, being a Built to Last company means doing everything possible to make the company better tomorrow than it is today.

The dimension most remarkable about Built to Last companies is their ability and willingness to simultaneously adopt two seemingly contrary objectives at the same time. Big picture and minute detail, creativity and rational analysis, stability and renewal. These apparently opposing forces working together is what makes companies great. They call this concept the *"Genius of the AND as opposed to the tyranny of the OR."*

Business Think by Dave Marcum & Steve Smith

When the financial impact is missing, any criteria (positional power, sacred cows, or political clout) can cut in and persuade people to accept inferior ideas that offer irrelevant solutions of less impact.

Without financial clarity, non-business people, non-business cases, and non-business solutions often win. True business leaders never let cash out of the door that doesn't strictly, ultimately bring more cash back.

Additional Resources

Please check out the following resources too!

www.MyRevenueRescue.com
Build a Booming Business In Any Economy!

www.MaidServiceMarketing.com
Steven's Blog, with Fascinating Tools and Strategies for FREE!

www.StevenRowellRecommends.com
Check out all of Steven's Resources and Recommendations!

www.CleanIsNotEnough.com/mastermind
Learn how to Double Your Sales, Triple Your Net Profits, and Retire in Three Years or Less!

www.retiremenowsteven.com
Grow the Business of Your Dreams in Record Time

www.ReconnectLLC.com
Steven's Organizational Change Consulting Practice

www.businesstrainingworks.com
Find Training, Consulting, and Free Resources on Leadership, Sales, Customer Service, Business Etiquette, Cross-Cultural Communication, and More.

Need a Great Speaker for your next event?

Steven Rowell speaks at 110 or more events every year sharing his expertise in Leadership Effectiveness, Leading Change, Accountability, Service Excellence and Building a Booming Business in Any Economy
Call Steven directly to book him for your next event!

800-268-8170